What Others Are Saying about Grace and Her Strategies

As I read Suzy's story, so many memories came to mind that I had to pray for God's peace to fill my heart. Unfortunately, the subject of your book is way too true. Too many churches are completely careless in their handling of church members' private experiences and information. From the moment I read "Suzy's Story," I wanted to read the whole book. I felt angry about situations like these that occur in the church. Once I read further, I wanted to find out how I could impress upon my own church the importance of privacy. The information is very helpful, and this is the type of book I tell my pastors about.

—K. G. Broomes

You are an amazing writer! I enjoyed it. I especially enjoyed the story about Suzy. As a reader, it grabbed my attention and I wanted to read further. The words are relatable, and you've done a great job with the comparisons of church and a restaurant. Not many people are creative in that sense, and you mastered it! Again, great job, and I can't wait to read more.

—Y. Randolph

Informative and enjoyable read. The church should be safe and secure, including valuable personal information. *Church Privacy: Who Cares? You!* is a great teaching tool for those in leadership structure and practice. This book is an excellent asset to any organization discussing mishandled information and the importance of privacy.

—April Young

This book is an eye-opener on how the privacy of members at a church can be leaked. It shows how detrimental this can be to members and even impact their spiritual walk, how this can give the church a bad reputation, and how it can even cause the church to have legal troubles. All of this was done using a creative and light comparison to a restaurant although a heavy topic. This is a good book to refer to before placing membership at a congregation and, if in a church, a book to refer to when helping remediate any privacy issues.

—D. Crowell

Informative and enlightening! I believe that this book can help churches that struggle with privacy issues, especially if the leadership is open to what you have to offer.

—S. Savannah

As I read the beginning of your book it took me back to my previous role as ministry director for a new church plant I served a while back. I remembered the importance of confidentiality that we instilled in our church team and employees. As I read further so many Aha! moments resonated with me. It took me back to what I did great, but it opened up a lot of things I experienced as a director of ministry that I'm now thinking *if I only knew*. Everyone running a church with a number of ministries needs this book. People we put in place to help others need to be trained.

—R. Pickens

I highly recommend this book to church leaders, staff, members, volunteers, or anyone involved in ministry. It helps give them a better understanding of what privacy entails and that it's much more than keeping someone's conversation private, but it also includes financial and personal information of churchgoers. Protecting personal and private information of your congregation, visitors, and donors is vital in order to run a successful ministry. This book will encourage you to re-evaluate your current privacy guidelines and understand the importance of implementing proper procedures. The analogies and biblical references are very insightful. It is definitely an eye-opener to a topic that far too often goes unaddressed. I believe that investing in church privacy makes a good ministry.

—Brandie Robinson

I really enjoyed this book! Though it was a quick read, I felt that it gave me a lot of information that was usable, and if I were a church member, I feel that this book would have equipped me with the right mindset to approach this matter at the church, full understanding of why this is so important, an idea of what I can do, and why I should do it. The book was very relatable and hard-hitting, yet maintained a warm and professional tone. I felt that it gave churches and my church (if I had one) a certain respect, whilst still holding churches accountable for certain practices that occur. I felt that it gave ME a certain respect, yet held me accountable for my role within the church. Grace strongly impressed the idea of prevention being much better than cure, and did this with excellent analogies and biblical examples. There was a sense of high stakes, and in turn this had me invested, despite the fact that I personally only see a church when I go to drop off food bank donations. The reputational, financial, legal, and spiritual risks associated with failing in the area of privacy stuck. I feel that if I finally found a new church family, this book would now be part of my decision-making process on whether or not I wanted to stay.

—Stefanie Thompson

Indeed! I'd never given much thought to or been introduced in an official capacity to this privacy concept at the church level. I absolutely feel this book can be useful to church leaders and members.

It opened my eyes even more to the importance of privacy and how it should be a major component of church policy. This is timely information, and if other readers are like me, I never really thought of privacy in the church context before. But it's needed if the church is to be effective all around. And members certainly should have the trust of leadership with whom they share private information. Grace offers fresh and new insight into the concept of privacy in the church and why it should be a priority at every level of church operation and for every person in the membership. While direct, the book is not bogged down with legalese, but keeps the content digestible and understandable, tying in biblical relevance along the way. I really liked the Suzy story right off the bat.

—M. Johnson

Your analogy about technology (or app) usage is relatable to me. I can't count the number of times people have asked me why I'm not using an app where my church gathers to communicate. Thankfully, I'm not being forced, but I'm not in the loop. I understand it may be a practical way to make announcements. I do believe that the old-fashioned way of making announcements should not be abandoned in favor of these apps. Sometimes I have to ask another member what is going on because I'm out of the loop. I found myself saying that I could relate to the analogies and situations here even if something similar did not happen to me directly. Namely, the stories about Tina and Lisa because the focus is on excuses used by church members who lack discipline. It seems like hardly anyone has ever addressed these concerns before.

—S. Spears

CHURCH PRIVACY
WHO CARES?
YOU!

CHURCH PRIVACY WHO CARES? YOU!

SIMPLE WAYS ANYONE CAN FEED THE FLOCKS, STARVE RISKS, AND DITCH LIABILITIES

GRACE BUCKLER

NAD
PUBLISHING CO

Church Privacy: Who Cares? You!

Copyright © 2024 by Grace Buckler. All rights reserved.
First Edition: Published in Washington, DC, by NAD Publishing, Washington, DC 20044.
www.NadPublishing.com.
Request for information should be sent to info@nadpublishing.com.

All Scripture quotations, unless otherwise stated, are taken from the Holy Bible, New International Version® NIV®. Copyright © 1973, 1978, 1984, 2011 by Biblica Inc.™ Used by permission of Zondervan. All rights reserved world-wide. www.zondervan.com. The "NIV" and "New International Version" are trademarks registered in the United States Patent and Trademark office by Biblica, Inc.™
  Scripture quotations marked (NLT) are taken from the Holy Bible, New Living Translation, copyright © 1996, 2004, 2007, 2013 by Tyndale House Foundation. Used by permission of Tyndale House Publishers, Inc., Carol Stream, Illinois 60188. All rights reserved.
  Scripture quotations marked (ESV) are taken from The Holy Bible, English Standard Version® (ESV®), copyright © 2001 by Crossway, a publishing ministry of Good News Publishers. Used by permission. All rights reserved.
  Scripture quotations marked (NKJV) are taken from the New King James Version®. Copyright © 1982 by Thomas Nelson. Used by permission. All rights reserved.

Author's photos: Teron James
Interior design: Tania Nadia

Publisher's Cataloging-in-Publication data
Names: Buckler, Grace, author.
Title: Church privacy: who cares? You!: Simple ways anyone can feed the flocks, starve risks, and ditch liabilities / Grace Buckler.
Description: Includes bibliographical references. | Washington, D.C.: NAD Publishing, 2024.
Identifiers: LCCN: 2023952589 | ISBN: 978-1-7369478-6-9 (hardcover) | 978-1-7369478-2-1 (paperback) | 978-1-7369478-3-8 (ebook)
Subjects: LCSH Privacy, Right of. | Privacy--Moral and ethical aspects. | Christian leadership. |
Church work. | United States--Religious life and customs. | Confidential communications--Clergy. | Data privacy--United States. | Christian life. | BISAC SELF-HELP / Safety & Security / General | RELIGION / Christian Living / General | FAMILY & RELATIONSHIPS / General
Classification: LCC BV652.1 .B83 2024 | DDC 253--dc23

Library of Congress Control Number: 2023952589

Printed in the United States of America

LEGAL NOTICE AND DISCLAIMER

Please note that the information in this book offers a broad application of privacy best practices, implementation, and goals. You are responsible for your own choices and actions either directly or indirectly. Your results will be highly dependent on your efforts, the scope of your data collection activities, and your legal and regulatory obligations. Individual church environments and applicable laws are different and require consultation with a licensed professional for assessment and insights. You acknowledge that the information contained within this book is for educational and awareness purposes only. Please consult a licensed professional for more customized guidance and advice that is tailored to your specific church and your needs. All effort has been made to present general, accurate, reliable, up-to-date, and relevant information. No warranties of any kind are declared or implied. Note that the author is not engaging in the rendering of legal, financial, medical, IT, security, or professional advice. Therefore, the reader acknowledges that under no circumstances is the author or publisher responsible for any direct or indirect losses incurred as a result of the use of the information contained within this book, including (but not limited to) errors, omissions, or inaccuracies.

Any company information, products, website addresses, phone numbers, or links printed in this book are offered as resources and for illustration purposes. They are not intended in any way to be or to imply endorsements.

Details and names in some anecdotes and stories have been changed to protect the privacy or identities of the persons involved.

Motivate and Inspire Others!

Share These Books!

Special Quantity or Bulk Orders
Buy 10 or more books for a 30-40% discount.

To place an order, visit
NADPublishing.com.

NAD Publishing titles may be purchased in bulk at a discount for educational, business, fundraising, event, or promotional use. Custom imprinting or excepting is available to fit special event or branding needs.
For general information, please reach us at NADPublishing.com.
Scan the QR for discounts.

Resources by Grace Buckler

Church Privacy 101

Church Privacy Team

Church Privacy: Who Cares? You!

To Una,
for being an amazing bosom friend.

Contents

Acknowledgements ... 1

Introduction ... 5

1. C'mon 13
   Does your church have the right theology but use it at the wrong times?

2. Church Is Like a Restaurant ... 25
   Is your church prepared to serve? Better yet, do you have delicious items on the menu, but are you always out of stock on privacy?

3. Don't Be the Weak Link ... 37
   Let privacy be in the limelight in your ministry because ministry is only as strong as YOU.

4. The Star Caretaker ... 47
   Become a mindful caretaker of private information because it's then and ONLY then that you'll see great results.

5. Do You Fritter Away Church Funds
on Lawsuits? 63
    You may think that someone is too "nice" to sue
    you or the church. Think again. This section
    will prep you, just in case.

6. Grow in Grace 81
    As your church grows, it must address
    manifold needs. It's up to you to apply
    what you've learned through an action plan.

Notes 95

Connect with Grace beyond the Page 99

About Grace 102

Ways You Can Engage with Grace
throughout the Year 105

Available Anywhere Books and E-books Are Sold ...108

Special FREE Bonus Gift for You 110

Additional Resources 111

Acknowledgements

Most of all to the all-knowing God who said, "Write down the vision and make it plain," and for giving me a Savior who taught me valuable lessons through this process. You are always there when I need you. I won't trade you for anything in the whole wide world.

Everyone who contributed is not enumerated in this acknowledgement but is in my heart for their vital support in both good and challenging times.

To you, reader, who is reading this acknowledgement, I see you. I had you in mind the whole time, and I hope you find this book more helpful than I ever thought. Don't hesitate to reach out.

To my editorial team, Callie, Joyce, Betsy, Gabrielle, and Stephanie, for blasting through my redundant scribbles to create a book. In all that toil you dutifully reminded me to take an afternoon off to observe National Taco Day. You're each a God-send!

To all who offered advice, direction, and approach. This would have been messy without your passion.

To all who gave their precious time to reading and sometimes calling me to vent their stance on this topic—

Church Privacy: Who Cares? You!

your honest advice, suggestions, and unfettered contributions forged the creative process and made this book richer.

To those who permitted me to quote their personal messages or correspondence. You're so much appreciated. To Teron James, thanks for the pictures.

My heartfelt gratitude to my feisty prayer machines who jumped in and surrounded me in the morning, day, and midnight to slay any possibility of me thinking, *I wasn't called to write this book or any book in this series*. Every writer experiences a period of faith glitch, self-doubt, setback, mistakes, bad news, and uncertainty. Boy, did I have a trailer load of those! But you saw the big picture and the value in this book. You pounded the doors and windows of heaven for help until this book made its way to the press!

Thanks to my family (Kiss! Kiss!) and amazing friends. I love you! My dear friends who understand my silence—Lilian, Lore, Loretta, Tori, Sheila, Kate, Rufus, and Georgia—and my teachers and mentors. You're amazing!

To all who offered their reviews and endorsements, I appreciate your every word and confidence in this project.

To my clients, business partners, and students, our journey together through many years of privacy compliance challenges has sharpened and polished me to help churches across the globe.

Thanks to my grocer, Jennifer, who kept me well supplied with unblemished avocadoes and Milano chocolate raspberry cookies during my solitary writing times throughout the pandemic.

Acknowledgements

To all the preachers, clergy, and church leaders. You wholeheartedly opened your churches to me. I respect you for listening to what I had to say and for letting me talk to your members about privacy. You felt their input had value beyond your own congregation. That's faith! You have no idea the privacy catalyst you've become!

To Ana, who toured me around Scandinavia while I was incubating the ideas in this book series. I extend that thanks to George Washington University School of International Studies.

To all the speaking engagements that have given me the platform and rekindled my humble calling to give back my knowledge to churches.

Grateful to NAD Publishing advisors. Lady Rhoda, your friendship and encouragement helped me keep what little sanity I came to this project with. You're a stunning book doctor!

And finally ...

To Pastor & former Professor Joshua Powell, Ph.D. Joshua Powell, who was the first of many readers to propose the idea of adding a small pocket guide to my Church Privacy series, you humble and encourage me to keep doing this work. I mean it.

That said, you all deserve a trip to Bora-Bora!

People aren't just coming for good sermons, prayers, and Sunday school. They seek healthy spiritual vibes. Dignity. And safe connections.

Introduction

*But all things should be done decently
and in order.*
(1 Corinthians 14:40 ESV)

Writing "*WE NEED PRIVACY*" in red marker on your church bulletin board seems *almost* contradictory because churches are places where believers are supposed to feel the warmth of *true fellowship*.

But I wasn't taking this three-word squiggle at face value.

Behind that expression, I was hearing, "Help us!"

For all I knew this could have been the desperate cry of a frustrated parishioner scribbled under the cover of night with hopes a church leader would take notice—that members desperately needed privacy. I wish needing privacy in church wasn't such a taboo.

Church Privacy: Who Cares? You!

Did you know rock-solid relationships are impossible without personal limits, trust, and transparency? Similarly, churches regardless of their size struggle to deliver a trusted fellowship experience without privacy rules. Privacy rules are the *dos* and *don'ts* on how to collect, share, handle, and manage members' personal information. Privacy is that healthy limit you place on others—what you're comfortable letting them know about you, what you want them to do with the personal information you give them, and if you want them to share it with anyone else. Without rules, chaos and disorder will likely fill up the pews. Let's look at an example of how unmanaged privacy can be hurtful and destructive.

Distraught over a relationship, Suzy hurried to the altar, crying hysterically. An altar worker with eyes of concern placed a hand gently on her shoulder. Seeking to better understand the situation, she asked Suzy to confide in her so they could pray together. Longing for comfort, Suzy whispered out her private struggle. When they finished praying, Suzy felt a wave of peace engulf her. She believed her burdens were lifted. Weeks after, she walked into Sunday school. Sister Jamison was the first member she hugged.

"I heard what happened at your house the other week," she said, whispering an encouraging Bible verse over Suzy's shoulder as she strolled to her seat.

Shocked, Suzy dropped into the nearest chair.

Heard what? Lord, how did she know? She doesn't even serve in any ministry here.

Just then a boy walked into the class, searching the room for his mom—who happened to be sitting a row behind Suzy. He reached over to hug Suzy. For a second there, a child's loving hug was both timely and calming. Until it wasn't.

"Miss Suzy, why did your husband hide your keys and lock you out of your house? That's mean!"

"Who told you that, Theo?" she asked, struggling to fight the embarrassment.

"I read it in my mom's altar workers form."

"Theodore Clement Thompson, how many times do I need to tell you to stay out of my business?" his mom said, shaking her Bible in his direction.

"Sorry! They're right there on the dining table."

"So what? Did I ask you to read them?" Her voice grew unnaturally loud.

"No ... but I'm not the only one, Mom."

"You and your brothers know better than that, Theo."

"Dad reads them too. Everyone that comes over reads them. The other day ..."

Suzy rose from her seat, afraid of what else the boy might reveal to the Sunday school class. "Enough! I've heard enough!" She gave the boy a soft tap on the shoulder and walked out.

A young boy blurting out her private business at Sunday school? Suzy's heart sank as she made the startling realization that his mom, Heather, didn't disclose this to him ... he read notes she left in the open—which was just as unfair, careless,

Church Privacy: Who Cares? You!

and disrespectful as her blabbing to Sister Jamison! The peace she had been feeling instantly evaporated. And anger took its place. Suzy felt betrayed but more so embarrassed that a minor knew something so personal about her. In that moment, she decided she could not trust anyone in the church again. *After all, in this church, leaders do the same—and who'll reprimand an altar worker who's been a member for twenty-five years? Report this to Deacon Cain, the director of altar workers? No. What's the point?*

    This wasn't Suzy's issue. It was a church issue. And it has probably happened to you—in different ways. Privacy is a serious need at church. People aren't just coming for good sermons, prayers, and Sunday school. They seek healthy spiritual vibes. And safe connections. The truth is, this topic should compel us to change.

    When these types of issues crop up, it's also a church leader's nightmare. Church leaders, I see you. It's frustrating. May I put my virtual arm around your shoulders? I totally get your hesitation. How do you solve this problem without sabotaging the relationships of the people involved—Jamison, Theo, Heather (her husband and other sons), and Suzy? How do you help Suzy heal or prevent her from taking legal action? Or bar one or all of these members from quitting the church? Is there a place or a person to whom you could send them to learn and foster unity?

    Tough. But don't despair. A few easy dessertspoonful chapters (yes, really!) exist to change this for everyone involved.

Introduction

Shall I show you?

If privacy is not already a priority at your church, I believe it'll be on your to-do list by the time you complete this book—whether you're a churchgoer or leader. In a few short chapters, you'll learn more about how most churches have been particularly dismissive about this issue. And how this cavalier attitude toward privacy has permeated relationships in the church circle—often turning brother against brother and sister against sister. You will

- learn how your church can be the exception and a raving champion of privacy,
- increase your awareness and knowledge of privacy,
- have clarity on the steps you can take and the resources you can explore,
- avoid privacy violations like the one Suzy experienced or worse, and
- discover fellow churchgoers' privacy needs and legal rights and the authority of privacy laws and regulations.

If your privacy has been violated in church, I'm so sorry. Please accept my hugs. I wish I could see you in person right now. No matter your role, I can't wait to encourage you more, teach you, challenge you, listen to your stories, help you find perspective, and support you. And while you're reading every word in this book, I'm praying that God makes these takeaways arouse enthusiasm in

Church Privacy: Who Cares? You!

you about your higher calling to be a truly caring brother or sister to fellow churchgoers and believers. That, like me, you will have a great vision for privacy in your church and press on until it becomes a reality.

An ignored sin doesn't become righteousness. Same with a privacy violation.

Sadly, misplaced loyalty in church is more important to some than considering the negative spiritual impact that betrayal of confidence has on the church community.

Fix the problem church-wide.

1

C' mon . . .

"**C**'mon, we're all family!" Minister Seagram said, raising his raspy voice in Suzy's direction as if his scolding tone would bar her from leaving. It didn't faze her. His refrain did little to dilute her hurt—if anything, it embarrassed her even more. All he did was draw attention to Suzy's response to a humiliating situation.

"C'mon, we're all family" is the problem in that church as in many churches, including yours. It's the reason people like Heather won't learn or take responsibility—it's nothing but a cheap justification for carelessness. Besides, Sunday schools typically have visitors. That's the whole point: church members and leaders not understanding the damages that privacy violations cause. Minister Seagram is not wrong. But his timing and tone are off. Right theology but wrong context. What do I mean by that? We're family, but Jesus handpicked twelve disciples he could confide in. These were a close circle he asked to pray with him and to whom he revealed himself in ways he did not show himself to others during his ministry here on earth. Jesus didn't air out his disciples' personal information when visitors or outsiders were present. One disciple betrayed Jesus's confidence, and it hurt the entire group of disciples.

If we're really *all family* as in 1 Corinthians 12:26—"And if one member suffers, all the members suffer with it" (NKJV)—then if Suzy's privacy is violated, everyone should be equally hurt with her about Heather's shameful mistake. Minister Seagram is right about *family*, but he forgot Galatians 6:10: "As we have opportunity, let us do good to all, especially to those who are of the household of faith" (NKJV). We all know Heather did bad, not good. Suzy is injured. Instead of empathizing—going after Suzy in the hallway with a box of Kleenex—Minister Seagram is gaslighting, indirectly calling Suzy's spiritual maturity and reality into question. What's his message? That it's Suzy's fault for responding to the hurt. How would you feel if your life's struggles were the centerpiece on a fellow church member's dining table? Now do you see what I mean?

What would you say to Minister Seagram? It might be tempting to insult him. But what would that achieve? Reacting would only escalate the problem. Hold off on calling him a monster—after I finish this point, you'll know exactly what to say.

"C'mon, we're all family" is what Seagram grew up hearing in the church. It's even led him to ignore his own

C'mon . . .

past privacy hurts. He thinks this approach should work for everybody. Sadly, it doesn't and shouldn't work. An ignored sin doesn't become righteousness. Same with a privacy violation. He needs to be taught. Teach him something he'll never forget. How do I propose you do that? Tell Minister Seagram to

1. Stop the bleeding. That is, use his authority to *contain* the problem from spreading further. Address everyone in the room by apologizing to both Suzy and attendees about what just happened. Ask those present to not repeat this personal and very serious matter to anyone else but to allow the leadership to address the problem. Also, he should explain that spreading the information will further hurt Suzy and ruin many relationships.

2. Go after Suzy. With Kleenex. Express *empathy* along the lines of, "Suzy, on behalf of the leadership I'm very sorry about what you just experienced. It should never have happened. It's embarrassing and hurts you deeply because you entrusted us with your personal information. I want to help. Please allow us to investigate and address this error. When can I or someone in our leadership call to check on you this week?" Minister Seagram should give Suzy his phone number to call anytime she's ready to talk. And ask that she let him know what can be done to make her feel more peaceful and less distressed about the situation.

3. **Fix the problem church-wide.** After he chats with Suzy, point Minister Seagram to resources you believe could help him and other leaders *prevent* or *resolve* similar privacy violations in the church, help them become more aware of privacy, and help them manage different aspects of privacy in their church community.

To better equip you to recognize privacy violations in the church and know what to do about them, let's look at another common scenario.

I regret ever having that conversation with Christal, Caleb thought and quickly ducked inside the men's room when he spotted a group of leaders coming his direction. He had been a member of a megachurch for fifteen years thanks to his childhood friend, Christal, who painstakingly invited him to the church. There, he had access to learn from men who were living their lives as great spiritual role models, especially Elder Little. You can't help but love Elder Little—a dad figure to many. Caleb felt right at home. But all that changed in a split second. Now Caleb was distancing himself from Elder Little and other leaders. He wasn't holding a grudge, but it was awkward. Too bad he couldn't unhear what he heard. Things weren't what they used to be. Especially the part where he used to look up to Elder Little and admire the elder's leadership, influence, and approachability.

C'mon ...

That had all gone out the window when he vented to his friend Christal, now one of the church's secretaries, about his nomination for a role he didn't get.

"Can't believe the leaders said *no* to me being in that role. That burns! I really wanted to serve!"

"Everybody else got their roles, I see!"

"I just wish they were all like Elder Little."

"Excuse me?"

"Elder Little!"

"Why?"

"Soon as I told him about my interest in the role, he prayed with me about it. He was really supportive. But I can't believe the leadership declined. I'm sure he's just as disappointed."

"You could have fooled me! Elder Little? Prayed with you, Caleb?"

"What do you mean?"

"He didn't vote for you! He voted for Lisa Holmes! I don't really care for her anyway."

"Elder Little? How are you so sure?"

"I can tell you who else might have voted against you. I was there; I heard all the back and forth."

"That's none of my business, I guess. Maybe it just wasn't my time to take on this role."

"What exactly was Elder Little praying with you about? Sure he wasn't praying for Lisa? Ha! Two-faced! You know what really upsets me?"

"Christal, you're getting angry. Let's just leave it. I'm good. Seriously."

"I'll tell you what went on in there and who said what…"

"It's alright, Christal… I don't need to know anything. I'm alright."

To prove her loyalty to Caleb, Christal didn't hold back a single detail. Even though Caleb understood this may not have been the right time for him to serve in his desired role (for divine reasons), it was tough processing the leadership meeting details from Christal. Caleb had grown spiritually but was still overwhelmed knowing how some leaders felt about him and their opinions of others who were serving in the church. He wished this conversation with Christal never happened.

Closed decision-making, opinions, and votes are private information—even state privacy laws recognize that and prevent individuals from being judged or discriminated against based on their vote or opinion. Sadly, misplaced loyalty in church is more important to some than considering the negative spiritual impact this has on the church community. Some loyalty allows members to violate the privacy of other members because they don't like them or are angry with them. Not liking someone doesn't give you the right to violate their privacy.

You may think, *I'm glad my church didn't hire a Christal.* But wait until you get your church's secretary mad. Or anyone else who knows a lot of personal information and opinions of people in the church—a preacher, ministry facilitator, elder, member, counselor, small group leader, and more. Privacy issues are not only a secretary's problem.

C'mon ...

We've all done wrong in this area to some degree. Admit it. We need privacy reform in church. Let's make privacy the norm.

What did Christal do?

I applaud Christal. For what? Glad you asked. She got a friend to commit to church for fifteen years—she understands discipleship. But do you see how her misplaced loyalty and damaging privacy violation could ruin relationships in church and send a Caleb out the door in fifteen seconds? I'm not applauding that. She doesn't understand privacy. She's not exercising integrity and godly wisdom, which are more important than competitiveness and loyalty to friends. Ministry roles take certain factors into account—gift, talent, assignment, suitability, timing, purpose, calling, readiness, God's direction—it's not a competition, and Jesus made this clear in Mark 9:34-35. I believe this also speaks to role, rank, title, and status in the church. Caleb already discerned and accepted this, but Christal won't let it rest. Here's what I also know: the day Caleb splits with this church, Christal will blame everyone but herself.

How would you handle this?

Would you propose your church fire Christal? You'd be justified—if she violated a church privacy policy that was put in place. But what would it say about your church

Church Privacy: Who Cares? You!

if you didn't have a privacy policy for employees? Or if Christal was never properly trained on handling this type of scenario and many others? Your church would be wrong.

Does your loyalty to your friends in church extend to violating the privacy of people you don't like? This is not only Christal's issue. This issue is a church privacy issue.

Does loyalty belong in church?

"Loyalty is not a fruit of the spirit."[1]

Christal needs to know this about her loyalty. C'mon, let's respect privacy even though we're family.

Privacy violation is not a fruit of the Spirit. I checked Galatians 5:22-23 and Ephesians 5:9 just to be sure. Sometimes we cleverly justify betraying others and violating their privacy. Privacy violation is one of the cleanest, most unsuspecting, justified, and safest ways to kill another person without blood on your hands. Our words contaminate or distract the hearers (Proverbs 15:4) like Christal's words did to Caleb. Other times they go undetected but are murderous like daggers. Jesus spoke of this in Matthew 5:22. Let's face it, we use privacy violation to warn someone about another person. It makes us appear caring and loyal when we say, "Let me give you a background on him because I don't want you to get hurt or be surprised." As long as you use it as caution, advice, or a sermon, nobody really questions your motive. It's perceived that you're doing a good deed by telling whatever

C'mon ...

the story is. I don't mean to get this deep. But it's time for a change. It's time to make privacy the norm.

My prayer is that God reminds us of Philippians 4:8 so we don't use each other's personal information as a weapon, conversation, distraction, or amusement.

Finally, brothers, whatever is true, whatever is honorable, whatever is just, whatever is pure, whatever is lovely, whatever is commendable, if there is any excellence, if there is anything worthy of praise, think about these things.

(Philippians 4:8 ESV)

Regardless of who you are to the church, you have a right to privacy, and your information must be protected.

> Business decisions and interests should not stamp out people's privacy needs or concerns.

> Unlawful tattling or sharing is also a business issue.

> A church is a service. It should take pride in offering stellar service.

2

Church Is Like a Restaurant

Imagine you are at Chipotle waiting your turn to place an order. You stare at the menu above the cashier's head. Your mind has gone blank, not quite reading the words because deep inside you already know what you're going to order. It's the same delicious meal that drives you to keep coming back over and over. Whenever you munch on it, it gives your palate a hit and lingers.

After standing in line at Chipotle, salivating for your favorite burrito bowl, you spot a white paper on the glass partition with scribbled lettering: "No cilantro" followed by a list of other ingredients you consider highly essential to a burrito. The sign ends with "Sorry for the inconvenience." Blah, blah. The rest of the words on the sign fade as you process this culinary injustice. All you can do is mutter, "I didn't come here for 'sorry.' This note doesn't help. It's not fair."

Once, I craved curry—Caribbean fare. I looked up a long list of restaurants. The restaurant with the word *mango* in their name was suggestive and persuasive enough. So I grabbed my car keys. My taste buds jubilated the entire way there. I grinned and walked in.

I stared at the menu for a moment and was ready to order. Then came the rainstorm on my parade. I overheard the cashier recite all the things they didn't have to a customer. *At this time of the day?* I rolled my eyes in disbelief and headed for the exit as did other customers who stood in line.

They were out of plantains and a number of other side dishes and even entrees. The cashier kept repeating the same tired script, "Come again!" with neither an apology nor empathy.

I'd say their customer care was unsatisfactory because it wasn't really conceding to the inconvenience this caused.

Even in disappointments, I still try to count my blessings. What if I had ordered something that made my stomach turn? I'd likely spend the evening sick as a dog. This is exactly how my stomach turns when I learn that a church has breached my privacy because

- They didn't have a privacy policy.

- Volunteers and employees were untrained.

- They didn't apply encryption on personal information in digital form.

- They knew nothing about privacy or about the ethical, legal, and regulatory obligations of collecting, using, or sharing personal information.

Even worse than this, leaders think privacy is IT. These churches are like restaurants who are woefully unprepared to serve their customers. They are, to say the least, out of plantains, cilantro, and good customer service. And their menu items are not up to par. They make people sick.

Let's compare churches and restaurants.

A church is similar to a restaurant. After all, your spirit gets fed there. You can grow from what's offered and your experiences; and when you exit the building, you can leave feeling better than when you entered. A church is a service. It should take pride in offering stellar service.

The Word of God is all good for us. There are some parts that we can't get enough of—God's promises and blessings are like a dark chocolate strawberry, chocolate fudge cake, or cranberry-apple pie. Other parts of the Word are like asparagus or broccoli—harder to swallow and not as pleasant to the taste (but will keep us spiritually fit). Those are the parts of the Word that talk about responsibility, obedience, accountability, and the law. You know, those parts we skim over. Consider this book like a generous serving of broccoli and asparagus (with love, of course!). I am giving you the healthy habits your church must absolutely adopt.

Like a restaurant, there's a whole menu of things to choose from in church. Conferences, webinars, workshops, courses, Bible studies, and sermons. There's also health, sports, fitness, fellowship, camping, retreats, and more. Certain items may be your favorite, so you get them often. The point is, at church you have a variety of "food" that can assist your walk with God, but for each plate—that is, church service, fellowship, or activity involving your personal information—there's a need to protect privacy. Unlike a restaurant, you're not really buying anything here. The church is not for creating profits. But even though your church is a nonprofit ministry, you still give your personal information and money through tithes and offerings, you get services and products, and get fed while you're growing and supporting the mission and others. You should be concerned about how your personal information is handled by the church—how it is protected from real money eaters: identity thieves or careless church workers. I thought about this lately while reading a short article entitled "The Church Is Not a Business" written by Keith Drury, an Associate Professor of Religion at Indiana Wesleyan University. One specific question gave me goose bumps. It reflected the missionary lives and journey of my parents and the scenarios I lived through growing up.

Church Is Like a Restaurant

> Where do you list the 14 hours you just spent in the hospital with a family while their son was going through open heart surgery? Or where will you list the "productivity effectiveness" of spending the next day arranging his funeral after the operation failed? In the church we defend such "wasted" time by saying we were not "making money" but "making ministry." Ministry is our bottom line. And ministry is a lot foggier to measure than money.[2]

This was spot-on. Those were hours I couldn't get back from my parents. But I don't really want them back. Investing in church privacy practices and education is also making good ministry, so don't look for a reimbursement check. Look for sparkly smiles and bright confidence from members who know you have their backs.

Churches serve a community of diverse people—in the form of members, visitors, donors, and partners. Regardless of who you are to the church, you have a right to privacy, and your information must be protected. That's the gist of this book.

Let me reveal further similarities between churches and restaurants so you can see the entire picture in context. Churches are similar to restaurants in the following ways:

- There's the church website with all the menu items of events, activities, and services to choose from just like at a restaurant.

- At church you conduct transactions all the time—donations, collections, offerings, and pledges—not for profit but so your church can expand its reach.

- Your cash or credit cards are processed the same way—whether written on envelopes, swiped on machines, or paid via payment apps or website forms.

- Because of the credit card transactions, information about you as a person is also processed—full name, contact information, ID—depending on what you're getting.

- There are workers who take your orders, for instance, what you tell them, prayer requests, event registration, and more.

- There are certain menu items you can order online and even pick up like carryout or curbside instead of paying at the door—e.g., books, DVDs, classes, workshops, and conferences.

- Monies are tallied up, recorded, and spent, and taxes are filed.

Even though a church's bottom line is different from a restaurant's, legal obligations are the same for

- the lawful collection, use, and sharing of personal information;
- information management and protection;

Church Is Like a Restaurant

- transactions or financial management; and
- communication management and ethical practices.

Church decisions or people's needs?

Business decisions and interests should not stamp out people's privacy needs or concerns. Churches must still answer to authorities about their business practices. If your church's business decisions about privacy are illegal or unethical, it can hurt people and put the church at risk. Think liabilities.

Again, when it comes to privacy, your church's interests should not outweigh members' privacy protection. Your church should balance people's privacy needs and the mission of the church. That's what laws expect from all organizations—churches included. As long as your church processes people's personal information—in computers, on paper, online, in video recordings, and verbally/orally—it's responsible and obligated to protect that information in line with legal and regulatory requirements. The last thing you want for your church is public disgrace because it mishandled personal information. It could cost the church thousands or even millions of dollars in fines and negative publicity. Imagine how discouraged donors, members, and potential members would be as a result.

Reflect

- How important do you think your church's credibility is to its immediate community, the people it's trying to reach, its geographical region, and authorities?

- Do you sometimes notice different ways your church could be risking its reputation because of how it handles people's personal business or information?

- Have you ever thought about how your own actions as a worker, volunteer, or member of the clergy could bring the whole church down?

- Do you handle other folks' personal information as carefully at church as you do your employer's or customers' information at your job?

- Does your church handle your personal information carefully?

The Point

These obligations apply to businesses, to the church, and to you and me. We're the church.

You're also like a key that opens your church. I mean in the sense that, in different ways, you provide access to personal information your church knows or processes about church members, workers, and visitors. Individuals with malicious intentions or criminals can use you to gain access to your church by exploiting your ignorance or carelessness. Churches and ministries need to follow specific principles for properly protecting members' and visitors' personal business regardless of how it is obtained and why.

The wise are glad to be instructed,
but babbling fools fall flat on their faces.
(Proverbs 10:8 NLT)

*Privacy is a right,
a need, a decision,
and a responsibility.*

Your diligence helps your church, you, and everyone.

Churchgoers care about their personal information and experiences.

Your church should balance people's privacy needs and the mission of the church.

3

Don't Be the Weak Link

I received a call from my electric company. It was odd. I normally don't get calls from them unless they somehow didn't receive my payment—which rarely happens since I auto pay electronically. Besides, two weeks prior when I called, they informed me I had overpaid by fifteen dollars. So, why were they calling me? I didn't need to pick up the phone, but I did. An automated voice alleged that my electricity was about to be cut off unless I selected "option one" and entered my "payment account details to proceed." Perplexed, I hung up.

I dialed my electric company and confirmed yet again that I had a zero balance. In fact, I still had a fifteen-dollar credit. My question was, "Why are you calling me?"

"We didn't call you. Our number gets spoofed by scammers all the time," the operator replied.

Church Privacy: Who Cares? You!

I processed that for a second, then grew philosophical. "All the time? Do you see that as an issue? What are *you* doing about it?"

I continued, "Do customers know? Do they realize they can get hurt by sharing their home address and exposing personal financial information to criminals—if they follow those phone prompts?"

"We can file a report ... if you want."

"If I want? Of course I want to file a report," I said. I muttered prayers and something unrepeatable under my breath, like "You really need training, lady!"

Can a church's phone number get spoofed? Absolutely! Can a church's directory of members, donors, and financial information get stolen? Yes. It happens often. Should church members know of these types of issues so they can protect themselves? Of course! But do most churches have the cavalier attitude of my electric company—with folded arms and an "If you want" type of solution? Yes. But they shouldn't. Protecting congregants' privacy in any form is your church's moral, ethical, legal, and regulatory obligation. Train people.

Your church is only as strong as you.

You're either your church's weakest link or its strongest agent against the mishandling of personal information. Bring privacy to the attention of your church or ministry leaders at the next meeting before a member or visitor fumes about how their personal information has been mis-

Don't Be the Weak Link

handled. The offended party could take legal action for a privacy violation or breach—not only against the church as a whole, but against individual members. Sadly, it won't be a hush lawsuit. Most likely, the media will broadcast your case as a consumer rights or human rights issue. What am I saying? Your diligence helps your church, you, and everyone. You can get mad or shrug your shoulders at the person who says they have privacy concerns. But what will you do if they serve you court papers? Has your church planned for these liabilities?

Consider the following: "Sixty-one percent (61%) of people (2,039) left their last church because of a conflict with another member resulting from gossip or strife that would not stop, was not true, or was not properly dealt with. They also marked a lack of hospitality and a lack of Bible teaching second or third."[3] Trust is everything. Honoring people's privacy is about building trust with them. Did you know that research shows a majority of churchgoers don't trust their church leaders?[4] Learn how to increase trust by managing needs and minimizing the risks of collecting and using personal information. It's just as important as taking a discipleship course or upgrading your computer skills. Learning about the privacy risks will not only be useful to your church, but you'll gain knowledge to protect yourself from mistakes that can lead to data breaches and privacy violations. From the statistics, I can infer that strife and gossip result from a lack of privacy discipline. If gossip abounds, the church is already on a speedboat to failure.

Church Privacy: Who Cares? You!

Privacy harms are not limited to utility companies getting hoaxed. Criminals can pose as technology companies that own the apps you use at church. They can craft emails to trick you into disclosing your personal information. Some technology companies don't have to pose as strangers to steal your information or violate your privacy. Sometimes they take your personal information in deceptive and illegal ways when they realize you don't quite understand your privacy rights.

It seems out of your control. I understand. But it's important I point out that, in most cases, technology apps don't steal data without someone giving them a foothold. Ignorance about good privacy practices and processes is a foothold. Most of the time, you have to agree to some permissions in the terms and conditions in order to use apps. However, remember that the majority of app users (you included) skip over the terms and conditions. You just push the button that says, "I agree," so you can quickly use an app or platform. Some tech companies exploit the fact that you don't read. It means they take advantage of your ignorance and your constant craving for convenience. That gives them a reason to help themselves to your personal information and, in most cases, your phone contacts—or other people you're connected with. Privacy is not a technology problem. Anyone can invade your privacy—it could be the altar worker, your church leaders, a traveling salesman, or a technology company. The value of your privacy doesn't change based on the invader.

Don't Be the Weak Link

Privacy is a right, a need, a decision, and a responsibility. You should be concerned and take responsibility, as should the church.

This may seem like a lot. Perhaps you don't know where to begin. Or you feel overwhelmed. I totally get that. In my humble church-observer experience, I've seen many privacy transgressions of churches. Sadly, the church can be very unrepentant and *undisciplined* about privacy violations—like an addict who is in denial. If you're in denial, privacy problems won't get resolved.

In what areas is your church transgressing?

Let me start with seven areas:

1. Obtaining or recording people's personal information (in different forms)
2. Personal communication (email, phone, social media, or surveys)
3. Sharing personal information—between individuals, departments, or groups
4. Storing and safekeeping of audio, video, paper, digital, oral, or computer records
5. Disposing of personal information after it's no longer needed
6. Purchasing of systems, software, or applications that pull personal information

Church Privacy: Who Cares? You!

7. Privacy training and awareness for leaders, members, and all levels of workers

Churchgoers care about their personal information. They want to protect and control how the church collects, uses, and shares their personal information. Which, by the way, is a healthy desire to have. By *undisciplined* I mean that privacy practices of some churches are disorganized. Unrestricted. Unplanned. Reckless. Inconsistent. Unsystematic. This mess can and does get people and church communities in trouble. Also, church members love to spread private information they know about other members, even when it's uncalled for. That's a monumental problem. Initially, this behavior came from a good place but has morphed into a personal privacy concern. Unlawful tattling or sharing is also a business issue. I detail this in *Church Privacy Team*. So how is this a business issue for churches? For starters, churches are huge consumers of personal information—but they are not always good caretakers of that information.

Consider this: How can you make your favorite dress or shirt last longer if you completely ignore the care label? And how do you care for an exotic plant without learning what it needs to thrive? How do you bake a chocolate raspberry truffle cheesecake for the first time without reading a recipe? Similarly, how can your church community grow by ignoring essential privacy needs of its members? Or by overlooking how privacy is handled across multiple departments and ministries? How can your church have excellent privacy practices, earn the trust of its members and community, and comply with privacy authorities if it doesn't read a book like this and put it into practice?

I don't know about you, but I don't want to see my tithes and offerings being paid out to the state because my church lost a lawsuit. I don't mind someone driving a nicer car than mine, but I do mind a successful plaintiff driving the latest Ferrari Purosangue at the church's expense.

Without counsel plans fail,
but with many advisers they succeed.
(Proverbs 15:22 ESV)

You don't need to have all the answers, but you do need to do your homework.

Never deny people services, prayers, or fellowship because they're concerned about privacy—work with them.

You could face legal actions for invasion or violation of privacy—even for the lack of proper processes connected to activities you do for your church.

4

The Star Caretaker

How would you feel if you were suddenly dropped from a ministry? You were given the cold shoulder and left out of the loop? That'd be a nightmare no matter the reason you were excommunicated. Timothy was kicked out for disobedience to ministry authority. Now, *that* sounded serious until I heard the whole story. Tim was unfairly chopped from a ministry because he didn't use a certain app. I kid you not, he was dumped after six years in the singles' ministry. Why? He shared with ministry leaders about a WhatsApp data breach affecting 500 million user accounts.[5] Tim felt it was necessary after ministry leaders announced the app to the members as the only medium of communication. He hesitated and wouldn't download the app himself by the due date ordered by the ministry facilitators. He was uncertain the app was safe for his phone and for all the personal information the ministry

Church Privacy: Who Cares? You!

wanted shared via the app. You would expect those facilitators said *thanks*, right? No. One facilitator retorted with a stern warning, stating something along the lines of "If you want to send or receive any communication from this ministry, request prayers, and fellowship with others, it can only be done through WhatsApp. We will no longer communicate with you or anyone via other means."

"That's gangster!" is how my mechanic would react to anything this brutal.

How do I see it? It's definitely bullyish. To me, the church's response sounds like a burden shoved on an innocent member to make them conform. It's unfair, uncompassionate, discriminatory, and disrespectful. I mean, what's the name of this place? WhatsApp Chapel? Sorry, usually when people report these things, I don't pry into church names, but for a second, it made me wonder. I'm sure WhatsApp wouldn't want to be associated with this attitude.

If you were that ministry facilitator, let me ask you this: What if God took back every one of your favorite answered prayers because you didn't pray them through WhatsApp? Would that be merciful and gracious? The point is, give people choices so they can still participate—combine email, apps, video, and text communications. That's what privacy is also about: choices and participation. Consider using email, the medium most people feel safe with. Don't condemn the innocent (Matthew 12:7). And never deny people services, prayers, and fellowship because they're concerned

The Star Caretaker

about privacy—work with them. I doubt that this ministry facilitator won't be emailing, texting, interacting in person, or calling other ministry members—please, let's be truthful.

Before you pick a single medium of communication for a ministry, do your homework by answering just seven simple questions. If you're a member and not a leader, respectfully remind your leaders or facilitators about these items:

1. What's your purpose for choosing this medium, and why is its use mandatory?

2. Will people be concerned about privacy risks?

3. Have you researched other options?

4. How will it protect privacy? Are you ready to respond to people's concerns?

5. What types of messages will be shared through this medium?

6. How can you help members protect themselves?

7. Will you educate users about the safety and risks of using this medium?

If having a single outlet for group or community communication is important to your ministry, have a web portal built so different groups can communicate there. How does that sound? This is inexpensive and will protect privacy and preserve relationships. Think about it.

Church Privacy: Who Cares? You!

Be a blessing in action.

You don't have to wait for the next general meeting. Be of service to your church now. Do you realize what a blessing you can be to your congregation by bringing up a handful of privacy concerns? You don't need to have all the answers, but you do need to do your homework. Even composing a checklist of existing practices to change or new ones to execute will help. A checklist of questions about protecting members' privacy is enough to get started. Why questions? Because if nobody knows the answers, you can make an amazing case for better privacy practices at your church. Communicate your ideas with power and zest.

Come on. Be bossy. With a saintly flair. Because that's when people will listen to you. Help your church take important steps forward. Then put a plan in place. And execute it.

Topics you can start with:

- finding out what's needed to protect people's privacy

- identifying what privacy laws and regulations require

- creating your church's privacy principles and basing a privacy plan on those principles

- planning for risks and liabilities

- connecting with privacy experts/consultants and finding training resources designed specifically for churches

What do people need?

People need to know that the information they provide to your church, whether in electronic or paper form, is protected and is accessed only by church workers who *need to know* the information. Members should have confidence and trust that their information is not being misused, disclosed to the wrong person, or lost.

What do you need to protect people's privacy?

Your church needs specific rules and policies that protect personal information in digital, paper (handwritten or typed), and oral form.

What plan do you need to make, and what's required by privacy laws and regulations?

Your church should research and get familiar with the laws in your state or jurisdiction and in states where your virtual members reside. If you know what's required of your church, dump that in your plan and whip it up into actionable, bite-size steps. But you need an expert to get you on the right path. Speaking of experts, before you get in front of an expert, put together a list of questions. For instance, think about the questions you'd like to ask me right now. In *Church Privacy Team*, the questions you *should* ask me will become obvious.

On which principles should you base a privacy plan?

First, your church should only collect personal information it truly needs. The collection must be necessary and lawful. There are other principles. Next, your church should handle this information fairly, protect it, and treat people as humans—with dignity and respect. They should only use the information for the purpose for which it was collected or processed. Your church should be transparent with members, visitors, and donors about how their personal information is collected, used, and shared. That means providing people with adequate notices and choices before collecting their personal information. For instance, members should receive privacy notices to better learn about how the church uses, shares, and protects personal information it collects. Does your church collect personal information for events, health purposes, births, memberships, and baptisms? Sculpt these principles into your privacy practices, policies, and plan. And create procedures and processes that will align with and achieve each principle.

What plan does your church need to have against unknown risks, and can it cut down liabilities?

Your church should figure out what could happen if it's not compliant with laws and regulations. Lawsuits? Fines? Prison time? Reputational damage? Lost time, investments, or opportunities?

I lead you through the steps you should take in more detail in *Church Privacy Team*, which covers personal information in your ministry operations, management, leadership, and decision-making at all levels. You'll be able to set up a program, come up with a strategy, account for the personal information you collect, create policies, and execute processes tailored to your church environment.

Church Privacy 101 is another companion to this book. It addresses personal information in relationships within the church and how improving the handling of personal information can prevent people from breaking up great, long-standing relationships or leaving your church because of unresolved conflicts. It also comes with a fun companion course that any church worker, coordinator, or leader can glide through on their own so you don't need to exhaust yourself making a case for good privacy practices. I got really excited and did the work for you so you can use the book as your checklist. If you're not in leadership, pass it along to someone in a higher rank than you in your church who will support your ideas and is committed to getting this done. No need to rack your brain;

Church Privacy: Who Cares? You!

Church Privacy 101 and *Church Privacy Team* will help you.

Handle one aspect of privacy at a time. This is not a solo act. Get other folks involved. Adults, youth, leaders, volunteers—it doesn't matter. There's something everyone can do to make this work. If you care about your church, you won't shrug this off like it's nothing.

> *Where there is no guidance, a people falls,*
> *but in an abundance of counselors*
> *there is safety.*
> (Proverbs 11:14 ESV)

Because your church collects and generates so much information about people, some of the fun topics I cover in *Church Privacy Team* include the privacy risks related to

- cameras in church
- data breach liability insurance
- in-person and digital prayer requests
- personal information in the cloud and emerging technologies
- state, federal, and international laws and regulations
- privacy policies and notices

Where do you think all the personal information you handle at church goes? It certainly doesn't die and go to heaven. Someone has that information even if you no longer have or use it.

That person can and will use the information for good reasons—but they could also use it for unauthorized reasons. The scary part is, it's not always someone outside the church. It could be the member with the cheeriest smile. Besides hoping that the church spends the offering on a new building instead of a privacy lawsuit, you need to help your church so it doesn't get blamed for the actions of malicious or careless people who steal or misuse personal information in church. Are you ready to do that? After all, fellow churchgoers could sue you. Yes, I mean *you*, not just your entire church. You could face legal actions for invasion or violation of privacy—even for the lack of proper processes connected to activities you do for your church. More details in the book *Church Privacy Team*.

How do you use technology in the church?

I commend you for seeking to learn about privacy. You won't regret it. Now let's turn your attention to my favorite subject again. Technology. I've helped churchgoers and members of the clergy from churches. Churches, whether small, medium, or large, have increased their use of technology. Churches impacted more people during the pandemic than any other time in their individual history—

Church Privacy: Who Cares? You!

even in congregations that were already megachurches with 2,000+ members or gigachurches with 10,000+ members pre-COVID-19. Live streaming and online communities have increased the need and complexities of managing personal information in church. Did you know live streaming increases online tithing and online attendance?[6] That's a big win for churches. With 49 percent of those donating to churches using their credit cards, which is a sharp contrast from past trends, it's evident that churches are collecting more personal information than ever before[7]—online. If your church doesn't ramp up its privacy practices, someone other than the church will be celebrating a win.

> *And we know that all things work together for good to those who love God, to those who are the called according to His purpose.*
> (Romans 8:28 NKJV)

What COVID-19 did to harm the church, God turned around for good (Genesis 50:20). Even so, you can't get too comfortable with technology. The same technologies and methods your church has used to its benefit pre-pandemic and during the pandemic now pose new risks and come with big privacy responsibilities and obligations. Plus, the old risks your church didn't quite manage pre-COVID-19 still exist. It's like the church has new

The Star Caretaker

shiny toys to play with. But the church needs to clean its room. It needs to organize the old technologies, figure out the risks of using technology, and come up with new strategies—especially for apps. Which apps do you use? Zoom, GroupMe, Slack, Snapchat, WhatsApp, Instagram, Facebook, Google, Microsoft products and services? Do you use Siri, Alexa, or Messenger? What old policy or process could you improve to help organize your apps and check them for privacy before you acquire new ones?

You might think apps are free, but who is paying? Who is giving up something for nothing? You. *Free* sounds like you pay nothing, but think about it.

You may be giving up a lot for a little convenience, and you may not be able to recover what you give.

Who is giving up control? You.

Whose information is going to get exploited? Yours.

Who is secretly going to change their privacy notice to pull back any promises made to you about encryption and your privacy? Some tech companies are. Who is earning $8 billion from collecting personal info? Not you. They are.

On top of that, you can also be affected with overexposure to spiritually poisonous, harmful, or unwholesome material. Think about all of this for a moment. I'm not here to bash apps; they certainly make our lives easier. However, we can't ignore the disturbing confessions of app companies. For instance, back in August 2020, Google engineers admitted that their privacy settings that would allow you to delete all your location information off Google maps didn't work consistently. Not only were the engineers unable to solve the problem, Google could also switch your location back on at its leisure, meaning your location wasn't truly off.[8] How do I know that? The state of Arizona sued. This, and many other cases, confirms that you should shift your attention to what's happening to protect yourself.

As I penned this section, a friend in church called me. She wanted help setting up her first Zoom account. Smart! She sought help. We went through the setup. Then she paused. Her tone changed when she said, "They're asking me for all this personal information. My first and last name. My date of birth. Should I really put my date of birth in here?"

"No," I replied.

She breathed a sigh of relief, then laughed. "What should I do?"

I responded, "If you've read the privacy policy and it doesn't give you the clarity or assurance you need, then change your thinking." She was silent, and I sensed fear.

I knew her birthday, so I was getting ready to ask, "What other month, day, or year would you have liked to be born?" But she interrupted me mid-sentence.

"I can use my parents' anniversary date?"

"There you go," I affirmed her choice. That date qualified as the beginning of her life—until this privacy policy gave her clarity and assurance that she could change that date. It's a trust thing. And although she is a lawyer, I knew she hadn't read Zoom's privacy policy yet—well, she has me. Do you recall ever reading Zoom's privacy policy and terms of use? Even if you did, were you shrewd about your personal information like she was? When was the last time you called a privacy expert when you were uncomfortable about supplying your personal information online?

Or did you feel intimidated and give in? We've all been there.

Can you imagine how many tech users in your church ask the same question as my friend—"What should I do?" Can you imagine how many give in? Do you have a church-wide tech and privacy checkup at your church? Or does everyone figure out technology use on their own? Does your church know a privacy expert they can call on? Take a moment to think about the answers to these questions before proceeding to the next chapter.

I am sending you out like sheep among wolves.
Therefore be as shrewd as snakes
and as innocent as doves.
(Matthew 10:16)

When was the last time you called a privacy expert when you were uncomfortable about supplying your personal information online?

> What in the world would influence a God-fearing member to sue the church or a fellow member for a privacy violation?

> Churches should not rely on the forgiveness of their members when it comes to losing personal information.

5

Do You Fritter Away Church Funds on Lawsuits?

Lisa told her story of restoration over and over in church. How she went from losing her cupcake business to God leading her to another business idea that didn't require dough and baking powder. Her e-commerce site reeled in six figures in revenue within ten months. How did Lisa do it? Lisa didn't hold back details. She shared everything that happened in between, like her near nervous breakdown and how she had to start over, stretching every last penny she had left. She agreed with the clergy that sharing her story would uplift others in a similar situation.

Church Privacy: Who Cares? You!

But when Lisa saw her story on the church's webpage published along with other testimonies, she was immediately uncomfortable. Yes, she agreed to share it, but why wasn't she happy? She wasn't worried about the testimony. She was worried about certain personal details in the story and how that negatively impacted her. Besides, some of the facts were out of order. She had privacy concerns. The church argued she should have had these concerns earlier. Wait. That's like saying you should have hurt earlier. It's like telling someone they should sneeze by a certain deadline. The church cited inconvenience. In other words, the process and deadlines for posting testimonies were set, and they wouldn't ask their website team to tweak any content—it was against the rules and was inconvenient. Lisa knew nothing about the *rules*, and even if she did, a person's privacy needs can change over time, and that's perfectly okay. Besides, there were errors. If you were Lisa, how would you feel—with this happening at your home church, not at *Newsweek* or *New York Times*? This wasn't worth causing her emotional distress over. She was trying to help the church. Her testimony was causing good traffic on the church's website and social media. Now she needed help. The clergy should have shown mercy, not *rules* (Luke 11:46), and helped lift her burden.

Processes and procedures should not focus only on the business interests of the church while overriding the privacy interests of church members. Both interests should be balanced. This is very simple. Ask Lisa which words or phrases she wants removed or reordered. Revise the copy and instruct the church webmaster to log in and tweak those elements. Overall, this task should take no more than ten minutes. And Lisa and everyone involved can avoid sabotaging their relationship—and getting into messy legal arguments and battles.

How about we dive into privacy legal battles in general? When you hear of an expensive and messy lawsuit, you'd sooner imagine it happening anywhere than in the church or between believers. However, messy and awkward lawsuits happen in churches more than you realize. And before you say it will never happen at your church, take a moment to learn why it could happen and how you can prevent it.

Here are four reasons people sue.

What in the world would influence a God-fearing member to sue the church or a fellow member for a privacy violation? I'm sure Mrs. Lindqvist and her church were just as baffled when she was sued by other church members and fellow volunteer buddies over an innocent picture they took together. I unravel her case in *Church Privacy 101*.

You don't have to be baffled if you're willing to learn more about privacy implications.

What are the main bases of privacy suits in the US and other countries? I discuss grounds for lawsuits in your companion guide, *Church Privacy Team*.

Let's take a quick look at the US. I'm going to keep it light, like I'm brushing melted butter on a pie crust. Don't let the legal terms intimidate you. It's plain and simple.

Church Privacy: Who Cares? You!

Here are the four grounds for suing a person or church:

1. Intrusion of Solitude or Intrusion Upon Seclusion (i.e., unexpected, unwanted, or unwelcomed entry into, observance of, or interruption of a private place, space, or situation where the person who is suing expected to be alone)

2. Appropriation of Name or Likeness (i.e., taking and using someone's name, voice, or photo/image/likeness without getting permission or consent and reaping some benefits from the use)

3. Public Disclosure of Private Facts (i.e., publishing private facts the public doesn't need to know, especially when the information being shared is offensive and can harm the person's reputation)

4. Portrayal in a False Light (i.e., telling part of a story that can give a wrong impression about a person—or flat-out lying about the person—causing them emotional distress and/or harm to their reputation)

What is "Intrusion of Solitude or Intrusion Upon Seclusion"?

Simply put, that means you could sue for privacy violation or invasion of privacy if someone intentionally makes

Do You Fritter Away Church Funds on Lawsuits?

public what you did. Or makes public something about you that you expected to stay behind closed doors. Imagine you're in a worship service; in between hymns, you sneak out. Understandably, with all that water you've been drinking, you have to go. You're in a bathroom stall. Whew! What a relief. Then you step out unzipped. You go to the mirror. You zip up and spend time there gazing at your face, practicing a couple of smile options before you go back out there in front of other people. You're in the restroom, so of course you expect privacy. Then you look up and around. On the ceiling there are cameras. They have captured everything from the time you rushed in until right then. Nothing on the door said you'd be under surveillance as you were using the toilet—otherwise, you would have curbed your urge. But you expected to be alone. A restroom is a place you assume a reasonable expectation of privacy. Sorry. Someone is intruding on your seclusion. It's offensive. As offensive as when a Florida family found a hidden camera in their cabin on a popular cruise line.[9] It's still an invasion or intrusion of privacy even if the cruise line did not place the camera there. As an organization, the cruise line should have been diligent. But it neglected to pay close enough attention to discover that someone had placed the camera there before the guests checked in to the cabin. As a result, the cruise line was liable. What's your church neglecting that it could be liable for?

Intrusion upon seclusion could be someone intentionally recording a private conversation they are not privy to;

Church Privacy: Who Cares? You!

someone going through your phone, looking for information; pointing a camera at your house and recording what's happening inside; or snooping on private records about church members and disclosing that information. It boils down to this: Something was not in the open. It was covered or private until the intruder made it public. And the act is highly offensive and causes the victim anguish or catches them by surprise.

What about if you're inside your car? You also have a reasonable expectation of privacy to an extent there. If it's a church-owned vehicle, forget it. That church car or van can be searched or accessed by the church anytime the church feels like it. It's your employer's property if you're a church van driver. So whatever you leave behind is on you. Inside your personal vehicle, however, is a different story.

The law in most cases doesn't recognize a person's expectation of privacy for something the person has intentionally made public or that is public record (i.e., social media, on your website, media interviews, publications, public directories, etc.). It's complicated, and the definitions of those grounds can vary by state.

Reflect

- Can someone claim your church was negligent and didn't do its duty to properly protect a member from a privacy violation or data breach? That is, it didn't secure information well enough or put privacy policies in place? Yes.

Do You Fritter Away Church Funds on Lawsuits?

- Can someone claim that because the church was negligent, it caused anguish or harm to a member or members of the church community? Yes.

- Can someone claim your church is liable for the mistake of a church worker and be entitled to damages? Yes.

Here's the interesting part. The person suing can still get paid if the court determines that your church was lax in its privacy practices. The person doesn't have to prove their identity was stolen because of a data breach or privacy violation, or that they lost a significant amount of money as a result. If your church was negligent, that's all it takes.[10] I don't know about you, but I'm not letting my church go down like that.

What is "Appropriation of Name or Likeness"?

Let's cut to the chase. This means don't use a gospel singer's or political figure's or anyone's image or likeness to promote church conferences, barbeques, or anything else. The person doesn't have to be famous to sue. It's no different from the rules for businesses. You can cordially invite a lawsuit if you use someone's image or voice for financial, personal, or church gain— even if you're doing a good deed and works of righteousness. The problem is, it gives the impression that the real owner of the likeness and image endorsed your efforts, when in reality they didn't. Remember, Jacob used his brother's likeness for financial gain (Genesis 27:1-40). Later, in Genesis 32, he said never again would he misappropriate anybody else's likeness. Too much trouble, and not worth the headache.

Reflect

- Have you ever assumed that because someone is in the greater community of Christ that they won't sue the church?

- Or that they'll overlook suing you or the church over something that was done for ministry gain, to increase attendance, or for church development? You would be wrong.

What is "Public Disclosure of Private Facts"?

This could be private information you have about someone. The person confided in you (like Suzy did in our earlier story). Or you just happen to know the private facts. Maybe you researched private facts about that person. And you published or publicized them. Have you ever read an article or blog or heard a sermon about someone and thought, *I didn't need to know all of that about her*? Or you thought of the person who made this public, *They could have said what they needed to say without putting*

Do You Fritter Away Church Funds on Lawsuits?

this out about that person? The writer may defend their actions by saying, "But it's the truth." But deep down you know they acted with spite. This is the type of situation where too much truth is bad. The public has no interest in those facts. Plus, it's offensive to the person these facts are about.

Do you sometimes defend what you're disclosing to a group of people who shouldn't know certain facts about a particular person? Do you use an excuse like, "Well, he told me that years ago. I'm just repeating the truth!" It's similar.

Far be it from you that you do nothing and watch your church be disgraced because it mishandled personal information by making private facts public. Just because it's true doesn't give you or your church the right to post or spread it. It's one way of showing you're being malicious. You shouldn't spread people's private facts. Period. Dare to gently tell your prayer group leader or preacher that his anecdotes or stories are a bit too revealing—everyone listening to them can figure out who he's talking about. And the person could sue.

Before the nativity story was cute, it was scandalous. Mary had no explanation for her pregnancy—other than the Holy Spirit was responsible as foretold. Her neighborhood was perplexed. Joseph's friends were not buying her divine visitation story. So they mounted pressure on Joseph to hurry and exercise his right.

Joseph had the right to air Mary's pregnancy as scandalous. It wasn't his. The situation was awkward. He didn't understand it. He was embarrassed. But "he did not want to disgrace her publicly." He intended "to break the engagement quietly" (Matthew 1:19 NLT). What kind of man is that? The kind that valued privacy even when he could have asserted how "right" he was or how he was cheated. Definitely "a righteous man." And from the looks of things, he was wronged. He had facts and could have taken to publicizing the private facts like most people did then, and still do today (shaming on Facebook, Instagram, you name it). Joseph was a good man who understood that publicly shaming someone is wrong even if you're right.

Reflect

- Has anyone ever cheated you? Or cheated on you?
- Did all privacy break loose because you were outraged?

Remember, the true character of a person comes out when things don't go their way. Sadly, for some, that true character will face a legal claim for public disclosure of private facts.

What is "False Light"?

False light means that someone has some private facts about you. Technically the information is true. But how the person presents it is misleading. Also, they may pub-

Do You Fritter Away Church Funds on Lawsuits?

licize or post a false statement but give the impression it's true. For instance, the person knows people think the world of you—that you're virtuous, trusted, supported, and extremely awesome. The person knows that if they publicized a certain fact or false statements, it might be misleading and misunderstood by people who like you and by total strangers. But that's exactly what the person intends to happen. They just placed you in a *false light*. They've caused people to misjudge or doubt you. What they've spread is offensive to you and is embarrassing—it hurts your dignity. But the person doesn't care about the emotional or mental costs to you. Such a person might be playing church detective, snooping around for facts that could be misconstrued to discredit you. They might even be attempting to get you kicked out of a church position or force you to leave the church. That's petty. Depending on the case, the court can determine if such a person acted with malice, among other factors. And if so, they'll pay for damages.

Reflect

- Have you ever shared personal information about someone but in a misleading way (maybe because you didn't like them or you were jealous of them)?

- Have you ever spread facts that other people didn't need to know about a particular person, and you portrayed the person in a negative way, knowing it would embarrass the person or hurt them in some way?

- Have you ever observed someone embarrass, isolate, misjudge, or mistreat someone else based on highly offensive and false information you shared with them about the person?

> *Get rid of all bitterness,*
> *rage and anger, brawling and slander,*
> *along with every form of malice.*
> (Ephesians 4:31)

Make no mistake. It's not just church members or visitors who could possibly sue your church. Donors, partners, and employees could as well. Regulators could sue for data breaches. Or sue if the church is not transparent—in its privacy notice and policies—about what it collects, handles, shares, or uses.

God hates a lying tongue (Proverbs 6:16-17), and so does the attorney general (AG) of your state. Your church prayed and helped vote your AG into office. Okay, so what? Sorry, the AG must fulfill their role as a privacy regulator. He or she is accountable to a higher authority the same way you and the church should be. "The Lord detests lying lips, but he delights in people who are trustworthy" (Proverbs 12:22). Based on my expertise, many privacy regulators across the globe seem delighted in the same.

Do You Fritter Away Church Funds on Lawsuits?

Will someone really sue your church?

I can't say. You can't control what people will do. But you should be ready. I'm simply stating reasons lawsuits can come about. Someone can use any of these avenues to drag the church or church members to court. What has the church got to lose? Precious time. Money on lawyers. Payout to victims. Credibility, reputation, and trust. What will the church gain? Free but negative publicity. People will talk. Especially when overzealous church members take to social media and post things like, "Please continue to pray for our church; we're getting sued for a privacy violation." Church members are quite capable of spreading the news—of course, they may not intend any harm. But, well-intentioned or not, spreading negative news such as a lawsuit will hurt the church. If you teach them privacy, they won't run to social media to pour out their laments about the church to the world.

You shouldn't resent your local news outlets for reporting a privacy violation that happened in your church. They're just doing their jobs—nothing personal.

Your church can cut down these risks. It will require a little discipline and being intentional about better privacy management. Humbly invite your church leaders to add privacy to the agenda for the next church business meeting. Then make sure you attend the meeting to talk about what's at stake. If you're in leadership, that's even better—work your influence.

Church Privacy: Who Cares? You!

Congrats! You've just learned very useful legal concepts in this chapter!
You deserve a raise.

Reflect

- Has your church ever lost your paperwork? The one you filled out with your full name, date of birth, home address, phone number, and email? And you had to fill it out again?

- If Starbucks, McDonalds, or KFC had lost that paperwork, would you have asked to see a manager? Why can't you hold your church to the same standards?

- Do you realize that, like money, the value of your private information doesn't change because of who is responsible for its loss? That the harm to you is the same?

The Point

Churches should not rely on the forgiveness of their members when it comes to losing personal information or not addressing privacy needs. Some people do nothing, either because they feel helpless, don't know what to do, or feel they have no control. But as more people

Do You Fritter Away Church Funds on Lawsuits?

become aware of their privacy rights, lawsuits might increase in your church.

The problem with merely forgiving the church is that the infraction will happen again and again. And it's difficult to track who last handled the personal information. For instance, when it comes to completed forms and misplaced forms, I've been told to "just fill out the form again." Even though I filled out two already—and they'd been misplaced. Nobody in church (except me) looked alarmed about the missing forms with all the personal information on them. Everyone just sighed and filled out another one. When I made eye contact with other members after yet another leader dropped the news of missing forms, they returned with dirty looks as if saying, "What? We're all in the same boat. Just fill out another one."

What boat? The boat of not questioning risky church practices? How did forms with personal information just vanish? By filling out that form again I was enabling the church's negligence. Not anymore! This time I was ready to topple the boat over, and I was getting off, right there. Enough.

How do we approach other members?

It was always the same deacon who lost members' personal information. His name is at the tip of my tongue right now. But angels are holding me back so I don't violate privacy. Two privacy wrongs don't make a right. I know. So I did what I had control over—within my rights.

Church Privacy: Who Cares? You!

I boycotted filling out any forms at church for almost a year. That didn't help. So I raised my hands to heaven and prayed, "Dear God, please deliver this deacon into my hands. I won't hurt him or anything like that."
 I just wanted an audience with him.
 I wanted to meet this deacon and tell him my thoughts about privacy and why losing forms with church members' personal information is careless and unacceptable. I wanted to make sure he wasn't a notorious wolf of a data-broker on the dark web—the online black market for trading personal information and anything illegal or stolen. What if he was posing in sheep's clothing as a deacon in my church? An auditing spirit came over me as I conversed with God. I wanted so bad to audit his home, his dining table, the trunk of his car, the back seat, the glove compartment, wherever he kept papers—everything. I was *angry*.
 I forgave him, but still, God made that deacon elude me every time I looked for him. I figured maybe God was saying this was a bigger problem than the one deacon and that I should do something about it. Not anonymously dropping a note on his car's windshield and calling it a day. But maybe the Lord wanted me to go beyond my church community. And write this book.

Be angry and do not sin;
do not let the sun go down on your anger.
(Ephesians 4:26 ESV)

I don't know about you, but I'm not letting my church go down like that.

Any issue that affects a church member is a church issue.

Leaders, members, and workers should be held accountable even at the risk of offending someone.

If you don't have time for privacy, you don't care about people.

6

Grow in Grace

Tina was warned she'd be dropped from or given a failing grade for the course she was taking in church unless, when she joined the class on Zoom, she'd be fully visible on camera. "That's the rule," the ministry director, Pastor Leah, insisted. The church leadership required all cameras to be on for participants to receive credit. Tina escalated the issue to the senior leadership—conflict loomed. A week earlier, Tina had had a major surgery on her head. Doctors advised keeping her head elevated to reduce gravity and swelling. Sensitivity to light is quite common for people who've experienced this type of operation. It was like torture when Tina tried staring at a computer screen, let alone engage with it for hours—"It burned like pepper spray," she recalled. Excessive swelling had left her face deformed beyond recognition. She described her hair as "a hot mess!" Doctors had sheared off some of her mane on the left side of her head. She didn't want even her beloved church family seeing her like this. Why couldn't Tina just drop the course and save herself and everyone the headache? Some people were quick to suggest what appeared to be the easiest way out—but not the best solution. Well, here's the thing. Pastor Leah already knew the situation. Tina wasn't trying to goof off behind the camera. She wasn't well. Something else we should consider, the healing aspect of this course. Tina stated, "When I joined everyone on Zoom, I didn't feel all alone going through this difficult time. I was distracted from my pain and from what I looked like. I didn't feel so self-conscious and discouraged. I could participate without dreading people would stare at me. My camera was off." Have you ever felt like you weren't ready to be seen? That's what privacy is. But Pastor Leah didn't buy that. "If I do that for you, then wouldn't I have to do it for every student who wants to be off camera?" she insisted.

That's not a question Tina should have to answer—that's a management issue. I see Pastor Leah's point, but she was wrong. Besides, she was not as powerless about this as she thought. Let's help her. How do we do that?

Upon being aware of Tina's health issue, Leah should have considered Tina's privacy needs regardless of the original class participation rules. Being courageous and

Grow in Grace

full of hope during life's difficulties didn't mean Tina didn't have a need for privacy. The church shouldn't force anyone to waive their dignity or their need for privacy—it's a personal decision. Rules shouldn't be enforced against people's privacy, but to help preserve it whenever possible. Based on this experience, one way Pastor Leah could handle future situations would be to create a set of criteria for people who request to be off camera for a time and treat privacy on a case-by-case basis.

Do you see the good that's revealed in this situation? Now the church knows their courses also give healing benefits to its members who need to be off camera for a time. Tina needs this course. Pastor Leah can now manage privacy needs easily, effectively, with flexibility, and with more empathy going forward. Tina will recover faster while earning credits from the course—with the camera off. That's what I call star caretaking!

A general lack of attention to privacy can give the impression that churches are bad workplaces, but that's not necessarily true. But there are important differences to be noted, and I explain this in *Church Privacy Team*. No worries, I'll give you a snippet of key differences between church workplaces and other corporate workplaces—the way I've shared with multiple churches.

Three differences: investment, management processes, and church expansion.

Investment

Other work environments invest more in privacy awareness and training to reduce harmful behaviors, namely, theft or unauthorized disclosure and use of personal information, while their workers are at work and/or working from home. The church is not a big investor in privacy training and awareness. However, the level of comfort and emotional and mental benefits church employees enjoy is covetable. Your church may never make the list of 100 Best Places to Work, but guess what? It could *be* the best place to work. How many places have you worked where your colleagues circled around you in a conference room and prayed you surge in joy and peace and burst with wisdom, knowledge, and skills to do your job with excellence? Church employees work together, pray together, worship together, and impact the world together. Team and individual relationships are sturdier because people hardly quit their jobs. But without investing in training and awareness, relationships and how employees handle their job responsibilities can turn sour, privacy-wise, because there are no clear expectations or limits. Now let's take a quick look at management processes and church expansion.

Management processes

The problem here begins when churches don't view privacy as a concern. Your church must recognize privacy as everyone's responsibility. Both members and workers should be held accountable even at the risk of offending someone.

Let's say an employee has turned in their resignation. Or a volunteer no longer wants to continue helping at your church. What happens to the loads of personal information they know or have about other people? Not only on paper in their homes, in their personal emails, and on their laptops but in their heads? Does your church have exit interviews or processes to check what these workers still have and what they need to delete, not use, keep controlled, or turn in to the church? Most churches don't have this process. Churches should have exit processes that require departing workers and volunteers to preserve privacy—no matter the person's status in the church. They can be a potential liability. If you think this is overdoing it, you need to count the potential cost of doing nothing.

*Or suppose a king is about
to go to war against another king.
Won't he first sit down and consider whether he is able
with ten thousand men to oppose the one coming
against him with twenty thousand?*
(Luke 14:31)

Church Privacy: Who Cares? You!

Church expansion

Most corporations plan for growth. Part of this planning is accounting for new privacy responsibilities, risks, and obligations the anticipated growth will present. Every church is praying the prayer of Jabez, although they may not realize they are. The prayer goes like this: "Oh, that you would bless me and enlarge my territory!" (1 Chronicles 4:10). Jabez might have been asking for more children, land, camels, crops, and oxen. We don't know. But like Jabez, every church is asking God for expansion. The church wants to grow—its membership, capabilities, technology, and finances. Great! That's how it should be. But while you're praying, realize the prayer isn't limited to *expansion* but is a prayer for direction and protection—"and keep me from harm so I'll be free from pain" (4:10b). Meaning, you might also want to pray that you take adequate actions as a good steward to prevent privacy violations, harm, or pain (to individuals and to the church). One adequate action is protecting personal information you collect as a result of your exponential church growth. Pray to apply best privacy practices. And nourish a sound and fun privacy program. Church expansion comes with more personal information you're responsible for protecting—personal information of church members, visitors, employees, and donors. It also comes with regulatory and legal obligations. No pun intended, but it comes with the "territory."

Grow in Grace

But first sit down and count the costs—the risks that come with expansion. Your obligations and responsibilities. Figure out what investments should be made to protect personal information.

As promised, that's a snippet of the differences between church and other corporate workplaces with regard to privacy. Let's do better, friend.

As I scroll through my tweets, I remember one of my replies to a mom and wife when she tweeted, "My privacy has essentially evaporated. How 'bout yours?'" The picture in her tweet spoke volumes—her five-year-old daughter walking in on her completely naked mom standing in front of the bathroom sink and mirror. In the child's hand, a tablet from school turned, showing her mother's nakedness.

"Mom, how do I stop the class video call?"

Short of words, I advised, "Designate certain areas in the home that smart phones, laptops, and tablets are forbidden ... you may even have to put up signs for your kids just to emphasize your rules." More on children in *Church Privacy 101*.

You've had your own awkward moments when you or your family members first started using Zoom and other conference platforms. Can you imagine how many naked churchgoers I've had to tell to shut off their cameras or put on some clothes? Interesting how many church attendees are still unaware the camera on a device is somebody else's eyes. And the microphone on the device is somebody else's ears. Once seen, you can't be unseen. And once heard, you

Church Privacy: Who Cares? You!

can't take it back. A little awareness goes a long way. Since your church started using Zoom, has it really sat down and thought about the privacy needs of members? It might come down to adding to your announcements, "Come as you are, stream as you are, but be dressed." This leads me to my next point before I wrap up.

Let's say your church's territory has expanded digitally with a massive following on Facebook, Instagram, YouTube, Twitter, TikTok, and WhatsApp. Prayers answered. Congrats!

But you're not quite finished. Members need to be taught how to safely use these new tools. They not only need to learn how an app works or how it solves a problem, but they need to learn how tech tools, while convenient, can invade their private lives. Here's my message to you and your amazing church community: don't pray for 400,000 social media followers or collect emails, prayer requests, and confessions there unless you are willing to protect people from technology and from themselves. Would you pray for a woman to become pregnant if you knew she would not care for the child? Don't pray for global expansion if you don't want to abide by privacy principles. Again, when it comes to running a church organization, you need rules to protect people and their privacy. Don't cringe at the thought of getting the church to pen an internal policy on privacy for every member to understand and follow. You need policies for different people—church workers, contractors, volunteers, and members of the clergy. I get deep into this in your companion book, *Church Privacy Team*.

Technically, good policy documents let people know where the church stands on respecting and preserving people's personal information. And it states what's expected of everyone.

Remember, privacy is an essential human need. If you don't have time for privacy, you don't care about people. The Bible clearly shows us how privacy impacts different aspects of our spiritual lives. It helps us stay within healthy and safe limits. Like a business vision and a business statement, writing down a privacy vision and mission is a prescription from heaven.

Good privacy practices in your church also keep everyone on the same page—legally.

Reflect

- Who is keeping your church community educated on privacy?

- If you work outside the church, is your employer making rules about working from home? Why do you think your employer is not taking any risks?

- Is your church community talking about privacy responsibilities that come with virtual expansion?

Church Privacy: Who Cares? You!

> *And the Lord answered me:*
> *Write the vision;*
> *make it plain on tablets,*
> *so he may run who reads it.*
> (Habakkuk 2:2 ESV)

A good-hearted privacy consultant, not necessarily a lawyer, can guide your church and help you create a structure and different types of administrative documents for privacy. I'm all for do-it-yourself. But get expert direction so you don't waste time. If money is tight, do it yourself, then call an expert to answer your questions. Good practices are not some sort of game for you or the church to dodge lawsuits with. It's about doing ministry the way it was meant to be done—from the heart. That includes looking out for the emotional, mental, spiritual, and physical needs of people and diligently protecting and respecting them.

The Point

The church is a place where people are cared for. It needs to understand how old needs have evolved, how new ones have surfaced, and the issues that threaten fulfilling these needs. It shouldn't ignore them or hope they'll go away. Any issue that affects a church member is a church issue.

Grow in Grace

I'm so excited you're reading this book. It makes my mission, which is now yours, a lot easier. Together, let's encourage our church organizations to be good stewards of personal information. Doing so will empower people and relationships in our church communities. Think about how you can start applying all the valuable information you've received in this book.

Imagine seeing your decisions blossom into action! This book is designed to help you plan your next move. Make a case for privacy with grace, passion, power, and pizzazz. Here are three moves to help you power up privacy at your church:

- Speak to your preacher, pastor, clergy, or leader this week about how the church can better protect members' privacy—share your own story and privacy concerns you've observed.

- Share this book with others in your church community.

- Pick up my upcoming books, *Church Privacy Team* and *Church Privacy 101*, so you can have the most comprehensive privacy education for your church.

As I mentioned, your next move can be as simple as booking that meeting with your clergy or small group and brainstorming ways to protect personal information to reduce risks. This means identifying practices in your church that need improvement and creating a plan to address them. Ministry is a calling to the business of humanity. Is

Church Privacy: Who Cares? You!

your church meeting fundamental human needs? For the sake of humanity, help protect people like Suzy. She needs her dignity, peace, honor, respect, trust, freedom, and to be heard as much as she needs sermons, Sunday school, and Bible studies. We all do.

Picture your church being that place. The place people are free from negligence, unauthorized sharing, misuse, and mishandling of their personal information. You'll discover this is possible if you decide to take church privacy seriously.

Being a star caretaker means not running away from a concern that scares you because you don't know how to handle it yet. It's understanding that running doesn't make it go away. It might make things worse. Privacy is like that.

If you don't read the care label, you ruin a nice dress. If you don't read and follow the recipe, you mess up a good cake. If you keep running out of cilantro or juicy fried plantains all the time, loyal customers become disappointed, feel frustrated, and no longer find you reliable.

Privacy is like that. A care label, a recipe. It gives you directions on protecting and satisfying people's fundamental needs. Running away from it or avoidance is also a decision. Avoiding any mention of privacy at your church, avoiding setting expectations, and avoiding people's need for privacy won't make privacy a non-issue. It won't free you or your church from legal and regulatory responsibilities and obligations. Decide. Be that star caretaker. Identify privacy risks and how to reduce them.

Schedule that meeting with leaders. Consult with an expert. Launch a dazzling privacy program. Run with it!

And while you're doing that, what questions do you have for me?

*Without counsel plans fail,
but with many advisers they succeed.*
(Proverbs 15:22 ESV)

Notes

1. K. J. Ramsey (@kjramseywrites), "Loyalty is not a Christian virtue or fruit of the Spirit," Instagram, July 5, 2022, https://www.instagram.com/p/CfpJE1PJpCW/.

2. Keith Drury, "The Church Is Not a Business," Drury Writing, Keith Drury, January 16, 2007, http://www.drurywriting.com/keith/church.business.htm.

3. Richard J. Krejcir, "Statistics on Why Churches Fail," Into Thy Word, accessed May 22, 2023, http://www.intothyword.org/apps/articles/default.asp?articleid=35969.

4. Pew Research Center, "Why Americans Don't Fully Trust Many Who Hold Positions of Power and Responsibility," September 19, 2019, https://www.pewresearch.org/politics/2019/09/19/why-americans-dont-fully-trust-many-who-hold-positions-of-power-and-responsibility/.

5. Craig Hale, "WhatsApp Data Breach Sees Nearly 500 Million User Records Up for Sale," TechRadar, Future US Inc., last updated December 1, 2022, https://www.techradar.com/news/whatsapp-data-breach-sees-nearly-500-million-user-records-up-for-sale.

6. Thomas Costello, "25 Church Statistics You Need to Know for 2021," ReachRight, January 27, 2021, https://reachrightstudios.com/25-church-statistics-for-2021/.

7. Milena, "Church Giving Statistics," Balancing Everything, last updated May 20, 2023, https://balancingeverything.com/church-giving-statistics/.

8. Tyler Sonnemaker, "Google's Own Engineers Said the Company 'Confuses Users' on Privacy Settings That Are Now the Subject of a Lawsuit," *Insider*, August 25, 2020, https://www.businessinsider.com/google-engineers-admit-privacy-settings-confuse-users-in-legal-docs-2020-8.

9. Janelle Griffith, "Florida Couple Say They Found Hidden Camera in Their Room on Carnival Cruise," NBC News, October 29, 2018, https://www.nbcnews.com/news/us-news/florida-couple-says-they-found-hidden-camera-their-room-carnival-n925691.

10. Ward PLLC, "Data Breaches Are Torts (Not the Delicious Kind)," February 5, 2018, https://wardpllc.com/2018/02/05/data-breaches-are-torts-not-the-delicious-kind/.

Connect with Grace beyond the Page

While Grace partners with organizations to achieve legal and regulatory compliance, train employees, and develop content, she is also available for the following favorites:

Keynotes, Talks, and Workshops

Grace delivers targeted content for groups and breakout workshop sessions that speak to church members, employees, and anyone in a ministry facilitator or other leadership role. Perfect for conferences, retreats, conventions, and meetings.

Leadership Privacy Development Training

In this lecture, Grace uncovers the potential of leaders and teaches them how to recognize and minimize privacy risks. She unravels the key principles that align their vision and mission to help leaders grow in how they care for people.

Organizational Privacy Consulting

Grace gives churches and ministries the tools, strategic direction, and tailored and customized solutions to help them reach their full privacy potential.

Divinity Schools, Colleges, Universities, Seminaries, and Associations

Grace gives talks under different types of budgets and programs including Training and Development, Learning Materials, Continuing Education, and Speaker Budgets.

Privacy Concierge Coaching

Grace maintains a select portfolio for leaders who need one-on-one coaching to maintain their own privacy balance while leading their church organizations.

See What Grace Is Up To

Request Grace to speak at your next event or for a media interview. Visit GraceBuckler.com/Speaking.

"Absolutely wonderful. I didn't realize how much I didn't know about privacy in the church! It's amazing as well as warm, educational, empowering, and relatable. Her humor keeps it interesting."

"She's practical, candid, affirming, and on point with biblical and life applications. Where was Grace when I was in seminary? It's never too late to unlearn the harmful practices I've learned for many years. I definitely wouldn't have thought about privacy in this way."

"Brilliant illustrations and thought-provoking real-world examples. I felt closer to our mission as a church thanks to her passion for fostering more trust, lasting relationships, and genuine fellowship in the church."

Scan this QR code for more information on courses:

About Grace

Grace Buckler is a recognized privacy, data protection, cybersecurity, and in-demand global privacy author, advisor, expert, and speaker. She has presented numerous topics on privacy for corporations, associations, business groups, colleges, universities, governments, and youth organizations worldwide. Grace is the founder of The Privacy Advocate, a data privacy consulting firm. Her fifteen-year career budded in the federal market where she served as a consultant and subject-matter expert both in the US and overseas. As an award-winning consultant for the United States Secret Service, Grace also served numerous federal entities with acknowledged excellence, including the Department of Health and Human Services (HHS), the Transportation Security Administration (TSA), the Defense Information Security Agency (DISA), the Department of Justice (DOJ), the Department of Homeland Security (DHS), the Department of Defense (DoD), and the Defense Counterintelligence and Security Agency (DCSA). Seven years of her career have been spent serving diverse markets, including Fortune 500 companies, startups, and nonprofits. She has authored articles for industry journals, functioned as an expert reviewer for US and European books in her industry, and served as faculty and an advisory board member for the largest global privacy association, the International Association of Privacy Professionals. Grace speaks regularly as a privacy subject matter expert for the Startup Law 101 Series.

Grace is a go-to privacy advisor, coach, and instructor for many leading organizations, law firms, churches, educational institutions, religious organizations, and clergypersons who desire to improve or master privacy risk management, gain members' trust, and achieve legal and regulatory compliance. In addition to her experience in cybersecurity, data privacy, and technical communication, Grace graduated *summa cum laude* from Albany Law School and holds a wealth of industry certifications including the Certified Information Systems Security Professional (CISSP), Certified Information Systems Auditor (CISA), Certification in Risk and Information Systems Control (CRISC), Project Management Professional (PMP), Certified Information Privacy Professional (European Data Protection Law & Practice), Certified Information Privacy Professional (US Corporate Privacy Law), Certified Information Privacy Professional (Government), Certified Information Privacy Manager (CIPM), and Certified Data Privacy Solutions Engineer (CDPSE).

When not wrangling privacy issues, Grace is a foodie! Some of her favorite street foods include Puerto Rican elote, West African boiled peanuts and roasted maize with plums, and Belgian waffles with strawberries and cream. She enjoys theater, traveling, discovering quaint towns, and trying new recipes from all parts of the world.

Ways You Can Engage with Grace throughout the Year

Speaking and Consulting Programs

7 Distorted Privacy Beliefs
Take Grace to Work Day
Take Grace to Church Day
Leadership Privacy Makeover
Grace, Teach My Parents Privacy
Single and Private
Privacy and Purity
Married and Private
Privacy with Kids and Teens
Senior and Private
Privacy That Heals
Beyond Privacy
Tough Questions, Tough Conversations

For information, visit
GraceBuckler.com/Speaking.

Stay in the Loop: Subscribe to Grace's emails for more spicy church privacy musings and for a chance to receive a free virtual privacy course ($699 value). Visit ChurchPrivacyBookSeries.com.

When you sign up, you'll also receive

- up-to-date info on her latest releases,

- downloads and other freebies when available (e.g., the world's first Privacy Prayer Poster), and

- information about when she's at a conference or church near you discussing privacy matters.

Get a Free 15-Minute Live Privacy Breakfast with Grace: This is a custom offer with a Q&A session ($499 value). It's for your church, your leadership, or individual ministry groups (singles, couples, teens, men, women, and seniors). This free gift is subject to availability. Send us your request via GraceBuckler.com/Speaking.

Take Grace to Church Day: You can take Grace to your church any day of the week. There's no place she'd rather be. Grace is available for your church's
- business meetings,
- employee retreats,
- organizational and operational consulting,
- leadership coaching,
- privacy courses, and
- privacy orientation for new employees.

Book Grace at GraceBuckler.com/Speaking.

Tough Questions, Tough Conversations: Got embarrassing, burning, frustrating, and tough privacy questions? We can relate. Send questions to grace@gracebuckler.com with the subject "Tough Questions." Limited to two questions per person and also subject to availability.

Available Anywhere Books and E-books Are Sold

Bulk Orders: You can purchase *Church Privacy: Who Cares? You!; Church Privacy 101*; and *Church Privacy Team* for church leadership and for different ministries in your church. Let your church and church bookstore know you need copies. You'll receive a discounted rate for bulk orders of 10 or more if you order at NADPublishing.com. You can also scan this QR code to save 30-40% on our books.

Thoughts: Did you enjoy this book? Was it helpful? Great, let's hear about it. One of your first steps in making a privacy difference starts here. That is, helping other people enjoy and learn from this content. Grace would appreciate you taking just a few minutes of your precious time to leave a review of this book—let Grace and other readers know what you enjoyed most, how it helped, and how you're applying or planning to apply your newfound knowledge. Imagine how many people you'd help by leaving a review on Amazon (even if you bought your book elsewhere).

Your Bright Ideas: Did you know you could email Grace and let her know your thoughts and the bright privacy ideas you've come up with that have helped you personally and at church? Also, if you'd like for Grace to feature your thoughts, experiences, and ideas in her next release or post, let us know, and we'll consider them based on availability.

Send emails to grace@gracebuckler.com.

Special FREE Bonus Gift for You

To help you achieve more success, there are extra BONUS GIFTS for you at ChurchPrivacyBookSeries.com.

Bonus Gifts:

Privacy Prayer

Onion Rings Privacy Template

7 Responses to Privacy Invaders

Secure your spot for a free virtual course.

Scan the QR code below.

Additional Resources

PRIVACY SUCCESS FOR CHURCH VOLUNTEERS AND EMPLOYEES

This resource provides secrets to turning volunteers into privacy allies who can protect your church and ministry from privacy violations and regulatory and legal issues. To access these quarterly tips, subscribe to the newsletter at ChurchPrivacyBookSeries.com.

Photo Credit: Climate Reality Project.

NEW *CHURCH PRIVACY TEAM* COURSE

Planning on reading *Church Privacy Team* next? Cool beans! Congrats! Now you have a ton of questions and tough church privacy decisions to make, and you'd love to have Grace on your side for your church's privacy journey. Don't wait, friend. This course is the best news since *Church Privacy Team* was penned. Join Grace in this fun and simple course. Let yourself be a beginner.

Let Grace show you how to get it done every step of the way. Secure your spot at LearnChurchPrivacy.com or scan the QR code.

NEW Expert Resources
Attend Grace's Church Privacy On Demand live privacy coaching. Wrangle privacy like a pro. And if your church would love to hack her caravan of phenomenal privacy experts, data protection specialists, and privacy lawyers in your area (including proven and trusted cybersecurity and insurance gurus), we'll provide suggestions to attendees.

Connect With Grace Online
Find Grace online. Help her protect privacy and spread love. Visit GraceBuckler.com and ChurchPrivacyBookSeries.com.

www.ingramcontent.com/pod-product-compliance
Lightning Source LLC
Chambersburg PA
CBHW060614080526
44585CB00013B/825